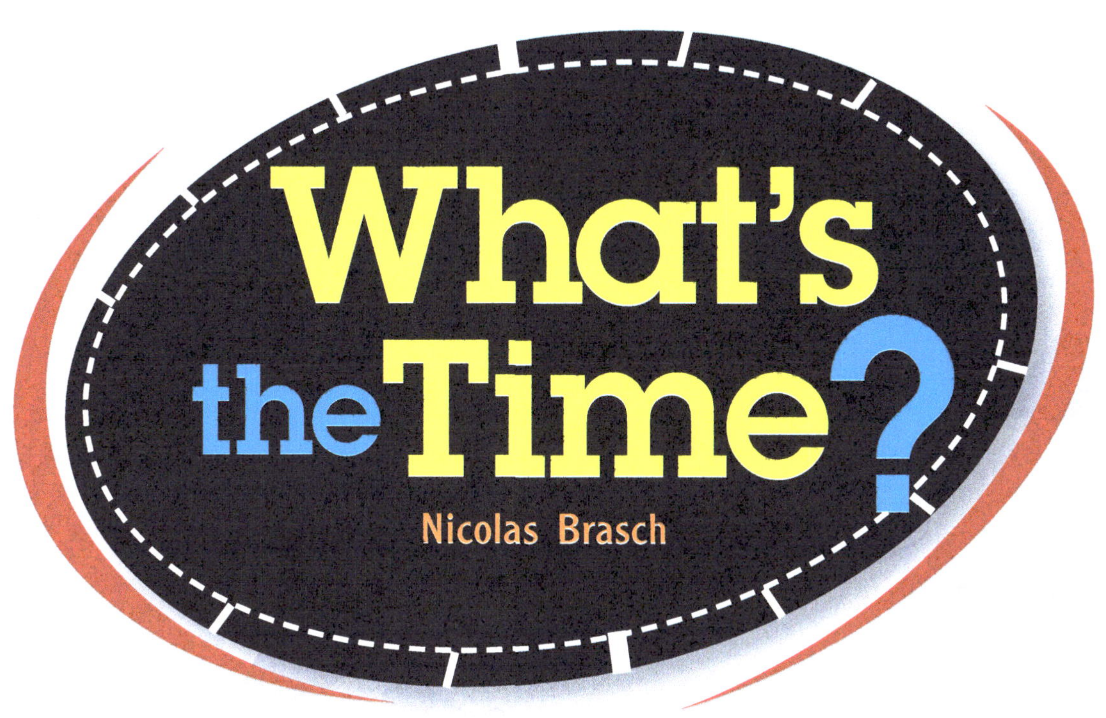

What's the Time?

Nicolas Brasch

NELSON CENGAGE Learning

Australia • Brazil • Japan • Korea • Mexico • Singapore • Spain • United Kingdom • United States

What's the Time

Fast Forward
Yellow Level 7

Text: Nicolas Brasch
Illustrations: Gaston Vanzet
Editor: Kate McGough
Designer: Vonda Pestana
Series Design: James Lowe
Production Controller: Emma Hayes
Photo Research: Corrina Tauschke
Reprint: Jennifer Foo

Acknowledgements
The author and publisher would like to acknowledge permission to reproduce material from the following sources: Photographs by Bill Thomas/Imagen, p.5; Istockphoto.com/Louise Aguinaldo, p.4 inset; Photos.com, p.4.

ISBN 978 0 17 012509 3
ISBN 978 0 17 012511 6 (set)

Cengage Learning Australia
Level 7, 80 Dorcas Street
South Melbourne, Victoria Australia 3205
Phone: 1300 790 853

Cengage Learning New Zealand
Unit 4B Rosedale Office Park
331 Rosedale Road, Albany, North Shore NZ 0632
Phone: 0800 449 725

For learning solutions, visit **cengage.com.au**

Printed in Australia by Ligare Pty Ltd
10 11 12 13 14 15 16 21 20 19 18 17

THE UNIVERSITY OF MELBOURNE

Evaluated in independent research by staff from the Department of Language, Literacy and Arts Education at the University of Melbourne.

Contents

Measuring Time

Time can be **measured** in hours, minutes and seconds.

Time can also be measured in days, weeks, months and years.

Parts of Time

Time is made up of parts.

1. There are 60 seconds in a minute.

2. There are 60 minutes in an hour.

6. There are 12 months in a year.

k-tick-tock-tick-tock-tick-tock-tick-tock-tick-tock-tick-tock-tick-tock-tick-tock-tick-tock-tick-tock
3. There are 24 hours in a day.
4. There are 7 days in a week.
May
Monday 23
Tuesday 24
Wednesday 25
May
Thursday 26
Friday 27
Saturday 28
Sunday
2006
MAY
23
WEEK 22
5. There are 52 weeks in a year.

Measuring a Year

A year is measured by how long it takes for Earth to go around the Sun.
It takes 365 days for Earth to go around the Sun.
There are 365 days in one year.

Sun

So it takes one year for Earth to go all the way around the Sun.

Measuring a Month

In the past, people measured time by the Moon.

The Moon goes around Earth. The time it takes for the Moon to go around the Earth is called a month.

It takes the Moon 29.5 days to go all the way around Earth.

But we cannot have 29.5 days in a month. So February has 28 days, or 29 days if it is a **leap year**. The rest of the months have 30 or 31 days.

Chapter 5

Measuring a Day

Earth spins around.

The time it takes for Earth to spin all the way around is what we call a day.

It is day when the part of Earth we live in is facing the Sun.

It is night when the part of Earth we live in is not facing the Sun.
night

Chapter 6

Measuring Time in the Past

In the past, time was measured by different **instruments**.

One of the first instruments to measure time was the **sundial**.

Time is measured by where the Sun's shadow falls on the sundial.

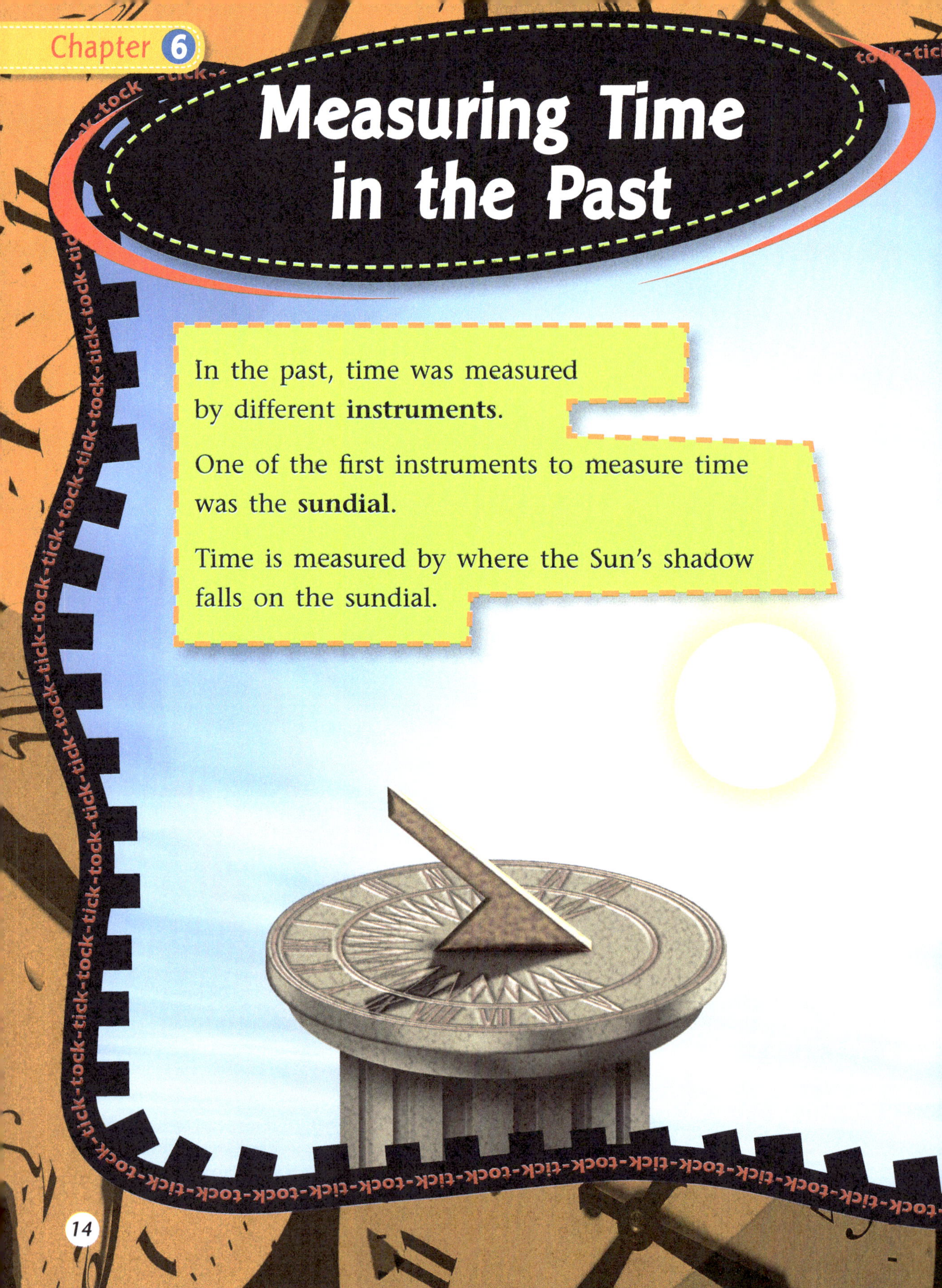

A sundial has marks for all the hours.
When the Sun is right over a sundial, the time is 12 o'clock.

Glossary

instruments	things used for measuring
leap year	a year that has 366 days. Leap years are every four years.
measured	worked out the 'amount' of something
sundial	an instrument that shows, or measures, time

Index